Becoming an Uber Private Hire Driver

Earn £40,000+ Annual Income and Work Flexible Hours

Stephen Hammond

Becoming an Uber Private Hire Driver

Earn £40,000+ Annual Income and Work Flexible Hours

© Copyright 2019 Stephen Christopher Charles Hammond

ISBN: 9781707556861
Independently published through Amazon

If you have any questions or comments relating to this publication, then please feel free to contact the author, stephen@stephenhammond.org.uk

Dedication

I dedicate this book firstly, to my wife, Ebun, and also to my father, Charles Hammond. I thank God for both of them, tremendously.

Contents

Introduction

Want to earn a £40,000+ annual income? In this book you will learn the insider secrets of how successful Uber Private Hire Drivers achieve this (and more). By using real life facts and figures from real life examples, you too can be earning a substantial income as a Private Hire Driver. Uber was the first to introduce disruptive and controversial technologies to the Taxi and Private Hire industry. Now there are other ride hailing apps as well, such as Viavan, Kapten, Bolt and Ola. As a self employed driver, you get to be your own boss and determine your own flexible hours of work that fit in with your own lifestyle needs. By making use of the information presented in this book, you will have at your fingertips all the necessary financial facts and figures that you need to get started straight away.

This book has been written for you to learn and understand how to be successful at maximising profits working in this lucrative part of the so called, 'gig economy'. This book has also been written with the digital age in mind. No longer is this business limited to local minicab offices running their operations with radio-controlled cars needing one metre high external aerials attached to them. Now new big Private Hire Operators have come into the market, contacting their Drivers remotely through Apps installed on smartphones. They are all backed by lots of big money to ensure they last as long as is needed to gain the biggest part of the market share, they can both get and hold on to. Uber, as market leaders, had six years head start in the UK on its rivals using App based platform technologies that interface seamlessly from Rider to Driver. In Chapter 6, I will talk about the minicab private hire companies that mainly do cash work. They also may use their own Driver Apps that can be installed on smartphones, but they work and operate slightly differently. I will show you how you can be successful in that market as well.

The content in this book is written from my own experience of over two years as a Private Hire Driver, and also drawing from the experience of others to show you how you can turn this business opportunity into the lucrative money-making income it is meant to be. The valuable things you will learn from this book have all been tried and tested in real life working situations. The information in this book will guide and help you to be highly effective and profitable as a Private Hire Driver driving for any of the App based platform operators. When you put into practice what you learn from this book, you will be among the top performing Private Hire Drivers. Also, this business is about making Riders happy and keep them coming back to use your services over and over again. I will show you how.

In addition to using the valuable information contained in this book, I would strongly recommend that you make use of all the information available to you from the various Private Hire Operators' websites as well as Transport for London (TfL). This book is written exclusively from the perspective of the Private Hire Driver's side, so that you can get both an 'insider' view and a balanced understanding of what the new business you are about to embark on involves.

The advice and information presented in this book will greatly aid to your business profits being healthy, your tips will be good and your ratings (where they apply) will also remain consistently high. That's assured!!

Finally, please do consider leaving a positive review about this book on Amazon, as it can really help others in the Amazon Community to be able to also benefit from it.

Chapter 1: Earn £40,000+ Annual Income

In this Chapter, I will show you how you can earn £40,000+ annual income using real life facts and figures from real life examples. Every new business needs a plan. Before engaging in any kind of new business venture you will want to know what the likely incomings and outgoings are going to be to help you to project the returns on your investment, so that you can know how much you can make from it as a business. Start-up costs in terms of registration as a Private Hire Driver and what vehicle to use are covered in Chapter 2: Getting Started.

Numbers of Private Hire Drivers in London

From the figures below, you can see that in London (with a population of approximately 9 million people), the Private Hire industry is simply huge.

"The number of licensed private hire drivers in London has almost doubled in less than a decade, from 59,000 in 2009-10 to 114,000 in 2017-18, while the number of black-cab drivers has fallen from 25,000 to just under 24,000. About 45,000 drivers work for Uber in London, according to the company." (The Guardian, 15 Aug 2018)

Figures from the Transport for London (TfL) website up to August 2019 state that there are currently approximately 106,150 registered Private Hire Drivers. Though the current number has significantly dropped, the numbers of applications are slowly increasing again. By contrast, the numbers of licensed Taxi Drivers in London have also dropped substantially to approximately 19,190. (licensed Taxi Drivers have consistently blamed Uber for a drop in the demand for their own market share of Riders.) The percentage of female Private Hire and Taxi Drivers is unfortunately approximately just over 2% in each of these licensed driver categories.

How Much Money Can You Make?

Based on my own personal experience, after the Private Hire Operator's commission has been deducted, the gross earnings you can expect for driving around the London area, will be £17.50 to £19.50 per hour (though this could be more if there is any higher demand pricing on at the time). Therefore, if you are doing a 12 hour shift, on a Monday to Friday and it is busy you could make up to around £200 gross. Some Drivers do work much longer hours than this. These figures are reasonably realistic and achievable based on real life working experience. Obviously, how much you get, depends on both how many hours you want to work and how busy the work is out there at the time. Also, if the roads are clearer, for example, in the evenings or on weekends, your earnings will greatly increase as a result.

Driver Earnings and Expenditures

Your fuel costs with a combustion engine vehicle (including hybrid) are likely to consume up to 12-15% of your gross income (depending on fuel prices and fuel consumption of your vehicle). Electric Vehicle recharging costs are around one third of normal combustion engine fuel costs and there are also no Congestion Charges to pay. However, to hire an Electric Vehicle may cost around £200 per week.

The figures in the table below reflect real life earning potential and costs to achieve a £40,000+ annum income:

Earnings for 60 hours per week at £18.50 per hour:	£1,110		
Less Hire and Reward (Taxi/Private Hire) Insurance per week:		£70	
Less Fuel:		£160	
Sub Total:			**£880**
Less Car hire* (If applicable):		£100	
Total Net Profit Earnings			**£780**
Per hour gross in real terms			*£13*

*7-8 year old hybrid car
Note: This table does not include Congestion Charges because it may not apply every day or in a driver's city area of working.

The above does not include cost for changing tyres, light bulbs, and any damages and repairs (that are not covered by insurance). Obviously, if you own the vehicle you will be using you will be directly responsible for all your own servicing, maintenance, repair costs, MOTs and TfL vehicle test inspections. The above does not take into account Electric Vehicles *(please see Electric Vehicles section in Chapter 3)*.

As a Private Hire Driver, using App based platforms for your work does give you a lot of flexibility but also provides lots of responsibility with it. This is because if you don't work then you do not earn. If you want to choose not to work on a particular day, that is up to you. Many Private Hire Drivers prefer this kind of flexibility, and as a result, many work part time only to add money to their earnings from an existing regular job they may do during the day. But it does mean that you may lose your evenings and weekends, because that is when Riders will most want your service. On the other hand, the flexibility can work brilliantly if you need an alternative work because you have children or want to run another business. In which case, private hire driving could be a real solution for you to make sure your bills get paid while you work on your other dreams and priorities. Therefore, it is up to you to think carefully about the number of hours you would like to commit to this.

Uber, in 2018, cut down on the number of hours of work a Driver could do with them (see section below, *Driving Time*). Prior to this, I once heard a crazy story about an Uber driver who earned in a week £1700 gross (before deducting costs). He worked 21 hours a day and slept in his car 3 hours a day. It is not necessary to go to this extreme to make sufficiently good money in this line of work. Even so, many Private Hire Drivers also drive for other App based platform operators as well as Uber, so they are not limited by the working hours Uber restricts their drivers to (or indeed how much they can earn overall).

Busiest Times

If the Driver App (for the App operator platform you are on) is busy, then it is likely you too will be busy. But this also obviously depends on the area you are in and how busy it is there at the time. There are times in the day when it is busier than others. Also, Monday to Thursday by around 12 midnight, demand from Riders dramatically reduces. The reason for this is that the vast majority of people are in bed asleep because they have to work the next day.

To give you an idea of how busy your day can be. On a typical Monday to Friday, the morning peak of 6 am to 10 am is obviously generally always busy with people going to work and night shifters going home. Then things can get a bit slow but pick up again from 12 pm, and then from there on get steadily busier to peak between 4 pm to 7.30 pm. Things can then die down a bit until 9.30 pm, and then build up again to remain busy till 12 midnight (or beyond midnight to the early hours of the morning on a Friday night). Friday and Saturday are generally busy all day, particularly into the night. (For many Riders, Friday is when their weekend begins.) The weekend then quietens down around 12 midnight on Sunday because of people going to work the next day (except when there is a Bank Holiday the next day). But this is only a guide, because it can easily get busy constantly throughout from the time you switch on the Driver App (or Apps) at any time of the day to the time you want to go home.

Driving Time

If you choose to drive for Uber, they set the maximum number of hours that you can drive in a set period. This is known as 'Driving Time', and the App shows how much Driving Time is left before the App will go offline. It is not meant to restrict you, but for health and safety reasons to ensure you have sufficient rest periods.

The Driving Time is set by Uber at 10 hours per shift session. Once the 10 hours have been expended, they will take you offline from the App, and you will need to compulsorily take a 6 hour offline break from the App before the Driving Time is reset again to 10 hours. Of course, at the end of the 10 hours Driving Time, there is nothing stopping you working on any of the other App based platform companies.

Driving Time is calculated as follows: Time taken from accepting a Rider request to picking them up, plus the time the trip takes to get the Rider to their destination. These two times are added together and then taken from the Driving Time left. So, for example, let's say that you have 8 hours 50 minutes left on your Driving Time. You get a request to pick up Rider A. It takes you 5 minutes to get to Rider A. It then takes you a further 10 minutes to take Rider A to their destination. So that will mean 5 minutes + 10 minutes = 15 minutes on trip time. The 15 minutes on trip time is then taken away from the Driving Time of 8 hours 50 minutes, to leave you with 8 hours 35 minutes left before you will have to take a compulsory 6 hour break from Uber.

10 hours Driving Time may not seem a lot, but does not include any breaks or intervals waiting between Rides. If the day is not very busy, it can take up to 14-15 hours to use up the whole 10 hours Driving Time. When it is very busy, it can take up to 12-13 hours to use up the Driving Time. After that, you will be tired, believe me! For this reason, I only do a maximum 12 hour shift, but on a Monday to Thursday I usually only do 7-9 hours a day, and then go home to rest and be fresh for the next day. Also, I only do 5-6 days a week, but that is just me. However, a lot of Private Hire Drivers do have no problem working 7 days a week, and some just do part time only at evenings and weekends. With this kind of work, it really is up to you how much you want to work and when you want to work.

Central London Congestion Charge
From 8th April 2019, all Private Hire Drivers that drive a combustion engine vehicle (including hybrid) and go into the Central London Congestion Charge Zone have to now pay the daily Congestion Charge rate of £11.50 (£10.50 Autopay). The Congestion Charge operates Monday to Friday, 7 am to 6 pm only. The only way to be exempt from this charge is to drive an Electric Vehicle (not hybrid vehicle). Therefore, the Toyota Prius (hybrid) car, which many Private Hire Drivers commonly drive, is not exempt from the charge. Uber charge a £1 toll fee to all Riders (except ride sharers) if the ride requires the Driver having to either drive through, pick up or drop off in the Congestion Charge Zone. This toll fee is then passed on to the Driver commission free. All other App based

platform operators also give Drivers incentives for having to drive into the Congestion Charge Zone. These extra fees and incentives do help to subsidise what you as a Driver have to pay to Transport for London.

In a shift you may have to go into the Congestion Zone many times. There is also a small risk that you may only enter the Congestion Zone once in a shift and still have to pay the daily charge. However, taking into account the above subsidy fees and incentives, I think it is definitely worthwhile going into the Congestion Zone, because it will expose you to much more work than not going into it at all. Therefore, going into the Congestion Zone is unavoidable to make your business successful, because you will then be available to do more rides. You may even find yourself never entering into the Congestion Zone at any time during a particular shift because the Driver App you are using has kept you out of it. My advice is to take it all on the chin and be available to work in the Congestion Charge Zone, because most Riders are in the inner to central London area, and therefore making yourself available to work there is much more lucrative for you.

Ultra Low Emission Zone (ULEZ) ULEZ
The ULEZ was brought in from 8th April 2019. The ULEZ operates Monday to Sunday, 24 hours a day. Any vehicle that is registered for Private Hire and not at least Euro 6 Diesel (generally registration year 2016) or at least Euro 4 Petrol will have to pay £12.50 per day to go into the Congestion Zone. Taxis and any vehicle that is wheelchair accessible and registered with TfL is exempt from the ULEZ charge. Many of the big operators like Addison Lee and car hire firms that specialise in Private Hire Vehicles have simply changed their

7-seater diesel fleet to newer diesel vehicles to be compliant with the new ULEZ requirements.

Hire and Reward Insurance

As a Private Hire Driver, you will need to have Hire and Reward Insurance. It's the law. It is a criminal offence not to have Hire and Reward Insurance in place every time you work.

The cost of this type of insurance can range from £50 to £100 per week (depending on your age, how long you have held a driving license for, number of points on your license and make/model and age of vehicle you will be driving, etc). Sometimes insurance is covered in the price if the rental company has fleet insurance. If not, insurance will be greatly cheaper if you can pay for 3 months in advance as opposed to only on a weekly or monthly basis. Then after one year you will be able to qualify for a no claims bonus discount on your insurance. Paying for only weekly or monthly renewable insurance means it costs more in the longer term and you will not be able to use them to claim a no claims bonus discount. Car hire costs can be from £100 to £200 per week (without insurance) dependant on the age, make and model of the vehicle. Also, many car rental companies, if they do not include insurance, may insist you take out fully comprehensive insurance. Although, some will accept 3rd Party only insurance. If the person or company you hire your car from is a small operator and the car breaks down, they may not have a car ready and available for you to use while the car is being repaired. Also, you will need to ensure you have suitable breakdown cover.

Roadside Recovery Insurance

If you are using your own car for Private Hire work you will need to get a Roadside Recovery policy from either AA or RAC that will cover Private Hire/Taxi registered vehicles. You will not be able to use a personal roadside recovery policy. Without the correct policy, the roadside recovery organisation may not agree to help you. To put things into perspective, if you do Private Hire work full time you may end up doing 30,000 to 40,000 miles a year. It is very likely you will need them to attend you at the roadside at some time or other. Therefore, if you rent your car for Private Hire work, you will need to confirm that the company you are hiring the car from has adequate roadside recovery in place. If it doesn't you will need to agree with them an independent arrangement, maybe each side pay half the cost for a roadside recovery policy.

Repairs and Damages

It makes sense to build a range of relationships with a number of different mechanics, especially ones closer to where you live. In London, the cheaper ones are in North London. The best places to go are backstreet garages under railway arches or back roads. There, you will find some very good mechanics and car body repairers that are much cheaper than obviously main car showroom dealers or mechanic shops on the high street. Also, if your car gets collision damage, backstreet car body repairers could be a very cheap and fast way of dealing with the repair, and therefore ensuring the minimum disruption for you before you are back on the road making money. The majority of these backstreet mechanics and car body repairers are run by people from ethnic minorities. If you are very good at making relationships with people of different ethnic backgrounds, you will be able to get better prices, but don't be afraid to negotiate, they expect it.

Chapter 2: Getting Started

Having looked at the more day to day financial aspects of this business in the last chapter, we now turn to how you get started. Here, we discuss about getting yourself registered as a Private Hire Driver and the different App based operators available for you to drive for. We will also be going into registering a car to use as a Private Hire Vehicle, and the pros and cons of the different kinds of vehicles you may like to consider using for your private hire work.

Private Hire Driver License

Before you can drive for any Private Hire Operator, you will need to apply for a license to work as a Private Hire Driver with the Public Carriage Office (PCO) department for the authority overseeing the area you would like to work in. If you want to work in Greater London, then you need to register and apply to Transport for London (TfL). Otherwise you will need to contact the local authority's licencing department for the area you want to work in. To apply to TfL, you can do this yourself by applying online directly to them or using an independent company. I used an independent company to assist in getting registered but you don't have to if you want to do it yourself. You can quickly find such companies through doing a simple Google search: *private hire driver license London*. These companies will add additional reasonable fees for their services, and generally do provide a good service. It may cost you approximately up to an extra £200 to use them (depending on what part of the process you need them for).

Private Hire Driver Requirements and Costs
To apply, you will need to:
- Be at least 21 years old.
- Hold a UK or EEA state driving license for at least 3 years.
- Have the right to live and work in the UK.
- Have a National Insurance Number
- Have Disclosure and Barring Service (DBS) 'Enhanced' Criminal Record Check.
- Provide a medical certificate of fitness from a doctor.
- Do a topographical (map reading) skills assessment.
- Have a basic *Level B1 English* qualification (unless you already have any UK qualification of any level).

The process through TfL usually takes around 2-3 months. The reason for the long time is firstly you need to wait for the DBS Enhanced check by the police to be completed. Once TfL have this and your medical report, they will then let you do the Topographical (map reading) test. Then once they have the result of the map reading test, they will then forward your application file for one of their decision makers to make a decision. Within a few days of that you will get your badge and license certificate to say you are a registered Private Hire Driver. The license lasts for 3 years before you need to renew it again.

If you do register with TfL as a Private Hire Driver then the following costs may be applicable for your application:

DBS disclosure application:	£56.85 (online) £58.85 (paper)	
License application fee (non-refundable):	£124	
Grant of License fee:	£186	
Post Office® Check and Send:	£7.15	
English language assessment (if applicable):	£180 - £200	
Topographical assessment (if applicable):	£75	
Medical Fee (to your doctor):	£50-£100	
Example approximate total:		**£500***

*Not including English language assessment

PCO Private Hire Driver application costs to Local authority areas outside of London will be much lower because the population sizes in those areas will also be substantially lower.

Registering as A Private Hire Driver for an App Based Platform Operator

There are currently a number of different private hire App based platform operators open to you: Uber, Viavan, Kapten,

Bolt, Ola (the list is actually growing). As a licensed Private Hire Driver, you will be able to drive for any or all of these. All the Private Hire platforms deal with 5 seat cars (4 passengers plus the driver). Uber, on their platform, call this option, UberX. Also, Uber as the biggest operator in the market and heavily influences what the other operators currently charge. In practice, they comparatively charge their Riders the same rates as Uber. Also, Uber offer 7-seater and executive cars, which not all the other App based platform operators currently offer as a specific service yet. However, they will accept these types of vehicles as part of their normal service. You can register with any of the App based platform operators by completing their basic online application on their respective website. However, you will not be able to drive for any of them until you have registered with TfL to be approved by them as a licensed Private Hire Driver. You will then need to drive an approved registered car by TfL (or the Public Carriage Office department for the local authority area you wish to work in).

The big Private Hire App based platform operators are:

Bolt: https://bolt.eu/
Kapten: https://www.kapten.com/uk/
Ola: https://www.gb.olacabs.com/
Uber: https://www.uber.com/gb/en/
Viavan: https://www.viavan.com/

More App based platform operators are likely to join this list. However, Uber presently operates in London and other major cities throughout UK. Ola operates in parts of: South Wales, South West England, Merseyside, West Midlands and

Reading. They also plan to operate in London soon. All the above operators have a presence in other countries.

Private Hire Vehicle
Whether you use your own car or rent or lease a car, the vehicle needs to be registered in the licensing authority area you would like to work in. If this is London, then it will be TfL. Uber provide a helpful list on their website of approved Vehicles that are accepted by TfL.

Any vehicle that seats up to 8 people including the driver and is used for hire and reward must have a Private Hire Vehicle license. The Private Hire Vehicle license costs £140 (with TfL) and lasts one year, and then must be renewed annually. Also, for the vehicle to be compliant, it will need to have a fresh MOT every 6 months. To register your vehicle with TfL for private hire work, the car needs to pass an inspection at one of the six TfL registered locations run by NSL, their contractor. The Private Hire Vehicle license inspection follows some of the basic requirements for the MOT.

The first time an application is made for a vehicle to have a Private Hire Vehicle license the vehicle cannot be more than 5 years old from the date of registration. License renewals can then be continued for up to 10 years from the vehicle's first registration date. From 1st January 2020, new vehicle applications for Private Hire use in the TfL area must be at least Euro 6 for both Petrol and Diesel vehicles (older than 18 months from registration date of vehicle). For new vehicles (under 18 months old) they have to be zero emissions.

If the vehicle has any deep scratch marks or dents or cracked lights, then it will fail. It is very important that you do an inspection of the car first, because even a single light bulb not working can fail the inspection. Also check the tread for all of the tyres to ensure they are not bald. The legal limit for the minimum depth of the tread in the central ¾ part of your tyres is set at 1.6mm. You can do a quick test to confirm if they are legal by inserting a 20p coin into the lowest tread depth of your tyres. If you can see the outer rim exposed then the tyre is illegal and needs to be changed immediately. If you are caught on the road driving with a tyre that falls below the legal limit then you could also risk getting 3 points on your license plus a fine.

Should I Rent, Lease, Buy or Use My Own Car?

This section mainly deals with combustion engine vehicles (including hybrid).

Use own car – If you use your own car, and work full time as a Private Hire Driver, then expect your mileage to radically increase per annum by around 40,000. If you choose to use your own car, make sure that it is neat and tidy and has no unsightly scratches and dents. Otherwise, it will be picked up and fail at the TfL Private Hire Vehicle license inspection. If you own your car, you will be able to claim from HMRC a business mileage expense of up to 10,000 miles per year at 45p per mile. If you rent a car you will not be able to claim this. However, whether you use your own car or rent one, you will also be able to claim back on all fuel expenses.

Leasing and Rent to Buy – The other alternative, is to lease a vehicle. The car can become yours at the end of the lease period provided you pay an additional premium sum at the end. Leasing a vehicle may also have mileage restrictions. Also, you may be expected to sign up to a 5 years agreement. The cost of leasing plus the premium at the end of the period, could mean that the overall cost would be double the cost of purchasing a new car outright, so do shop around. Also, with leasing, you may be responsible for cost of maintenance for the car. It is therefore vital to ask lots of questions and read the small print. You will need to do your research to work out what is best for you. Rent to Buy schemes work in a similar way to lease schemes. I don't think they are good value for money. For all the money you would be spending, to me it makes sense to just rent only, and save up for a deposit and then get a straightforward car loan from your bank or other similar loan finance company. However, if this is the option you would like to try, you find many of these companies listed on Google.

<u>Buy a car</u> – If you buy a car, better to buy it outright or try to get a 2 (maximum 3) year car loan (or hire purchase) if you can. That way you can clear the debt early and the car will be yours once the debt has been settled. Then after 2-3 years immediately sell the car once it is fully yours. Also, there is little point in buying a brand new car. You will not earn any extra for doing so unless it is an executive type model. Try to buy a car that is 3-4 years old, that is clean and tidy and scratch/dent free, and which has <u>low mileage</u>. You will be responsible for all maintenance and repairs.

<u>Rent a car</u> - Renting a vehicle is very easy, quick and least hassle option. You may be expected to pay a deposit of between 1-4 weeks (depending on the age and type of car),

and the equivalent of 1-4 weeks rent in advance. Also, some companies have their own fleet insurance. Those that don't will expect you to get your own insurance. Some companies expect you to get fully comprehensive insurance, and some will accept third party only. You will still be liable for light bulbs, oil top ups and tyres changes. They will deal with maintenance and servicing, but will charge you for damage and repairs if it goes outside of insurance claims. You can find vehicles available for rent on Gumtree or by putting in a Google search, such as: *pco car hire London*.

Electric Vehicles
When you have an Electric Vehicle, you will save on not having to pay for the Congestion Charge, and if you drive with Uber you will also still benefit from the extra £1 every time you have to either pick up, drop off or drive through the Congestion Charge Zone. (The other App based platform operators all have similar schemes and incentives as well.) The extra monies that you will receive will make the Private Hire business you are entering into even more rewarding for you. However, my advice is to buy either a brand new or nearly new (with low mileage) Electric Vehicle (so that it should be covered by the dealer's warranty) or rent one, but renting an Electric Vehicle can cost around £200 per week. These vehicles can still break down and there are hardly any mechanics that will be able to help you, except approved car dealerships for the make of the car.

If you go with Uber, they charge Riders an additional 15p per mile as part of their Clean Air Plan initiative, which is then passed on to you as part of the fare when you have an Electric Vehicle. If an Uber Driver does not have an Electric Vehicle, then the 15p per mile accumulated goes into a fund for the Driver to be used for acquiring an Electric Vehicle at a later date. Uber have external partners that they have negotiated with to make use of the accumulated Clean Air Plan money to offset the cost of getting an Electric Vehicle for their Drivers.

With Electric Vehicles there would be no fuel to pay for. However, there still would be the cost of recharging on a daily basis. To get a good understanding of the charging costs for Electric Vehicles please check out pod-point.com website. Electric Vehicles currently offer very limited real world mileage range. For example, the Nissan Leaf (2018) real world mileage range is around 150 miles. This is just on the toleration border for Private Hire work (but perhaps not advisable for long distance trips). Also, using the Air Con is a battery drainer. Recharging costs are approximately a third of fuel costs, and there is no Congestion Charge to pay. If you were to rent an Electric Vehicle this could mean a saving in weekly costs by a third in comparison to renting a combustion engine type vehicle (including hybrid). It is difficult at the moment to recommend using an Electric Car for private hire work because of the current limited mileage range, but that will obviously change as technology improves to overcome this limitation. In the meantime, there are many Private Hire Drivers that currently do drive Electric Vehicles and who are satisfied with them. Also, Uber in London has an intention to have fully Electric Vehicles working on their App by 2025. It clearly is a personal choice on whether to use an Electric Vehicle now or wait, but it is equally inevitable that one way or the other we will all be driving Electric Vehicles (or other vehicle that is zero emissions powered) at some point in the near future.

7-Seater and Executive Vehicles

If you are hoping to do either 7-seater or executive work then this will attract higher fares, and therefore higher earnings for you. However, not all App based platform operators offer these specific vehicle services. But all accept these types of vehicles on their App platforms as part of their normal standard service.

<u>7 Seaters</u> – On the Uber platform this type of vehicle relates to their UberXL service (but does not include Toyota Prius Plus 7-seater). If you have a vehicle that qualifies for UberXL, you may only end up doing around 2-3 UberXL trips a day with them in addition to UberX and UberPOOL (ride sharing). Unless you have your own 7-seater vehicle already or you specifically want a 7-seater, it may not be worthwhile getting such a big vehicle. Just to add, most of the Addison Lee private hire vehicles are 7 seaters. However, if you choose to join them, you will be expected to drive for them on an exclusive basis only. All local minicab firms accept Toyota Prius Plus as a 7-seater vehicle.

<u>Executive Service</u> – This service relates to high end executive type vehicles such as Mercedes Benz (E and S class) and BMW (5 and 7 series). A vehicle used for executive work should not be more than 3 years old from registration. This is typical policy throughout the private hire industry.

Uber and Bolt offer executive vehicles on their App platforms. Besides doing executive trips you would also be expected to do standard service trips as well. This is because providing Executive Vehicles are not part of either of these operators' core business. To be accepted by Uber as an UberExec driver, you will have to have completed at least 10,000 trips with them and have a rating of 4.85. To accomplish this little feat will mean you will have worked for Uber for at least 2 years.

If you already have an executive vehicle, it may be worth considering mixing working with any of the App based platform operators as well as doing work for some local minicab firms who may occasionally take pre-booking requests for executive type cars. If you want to specifically do chauffeuring work, there are a lot of chauffeur companies out there that will be glad to hear from you. However, they prefer people who already have existing experience as a Private Hire Driver. Some of these companies either require you to have your own executive vehicle or may offer to hire you one of their own. This kind of working requires men and women to have clean groomed appearance with smart suit attire.

8-Seater Vehicles
All App based platform operators accept 8 seat vehicles as part of their normal standard service. However, Uber will also accept them for their UberXL service as well. Also, vehicles, such as 8 seaters are largely van type manufacturer conversions that are more than 2 metres high/wide (and except for taxis) are not allowed through the London Rotherhithe Tunnel. Unless you are going to do Local minicab work, they may not be worth it for specifically App based platform operator work.

TfL Public Carriage Office (PCO) Inspectors

All authorities in the UK are expected to have PCO inspectors that will make random checks on both Hackney Carriage (Taxi) and Private Hire Drivers and the Vehicles they are driving in. TfL, and sometimes in conjunction with the police as well, do random road side inspections most typically at airports and railway stations. The reason why I am stating this is because TfL inspectors can really be anywhere at anytime. You need to be aware of this. They can legally pull you over to do an inspection at anytime, irrespective of whether or not you have any passengers. I have had passengers on board a few times when it has happened.

The things PCO inspectors most commonly look out for are:
- Private Hire Driver must be wearing their ID badge
- Private Hire Vehicle must have license visible. (If vehicle is registered with TfL, license discs must be on display on front and back windows)
- Valid Hire and Reward insurance
- MOT not more than 6 months old
- All lights are working
- Tyres are at the correct legal depth of tread

If at the time of a TfL's PCO road side inspection, 2 or more lights are not working then they can make an order for you to have your vehicle do a fresh MOT. It therefore makes sense to check you lights as well as your tyres tread every few days.

Which Mobile Phone

To work as a Private Hire Driver, you will need a mobile smartphone with ideally the following minimum specifications: 5 inch screen, 4G network, 3GB RAM, 3000mAh battery and a monthly data plan of at least 10GB. It is also good to have a power bank with you in case of emergencies. You will also need a car charger plug and spare charging cables for your phone. Charging cables do not last long in private hire work. I go through a new one every 1-2 months. Android phones do not drain the battery as quickly as iPhones. Sorry if that sounds tough to hear for iPhone users but that is the reality.

Insurance – Loading Up Document to the App

Most insurance brokers that specialise in hire and reward insurance may upload the insurance certificate automatically to the Driver App you are driving for. But they are not always fast or efficient. I have found it is always easier and quicker to upload directly myself. But the Driver App you are using may not accept PDF uploads on their App. To get around this, I use an App called PDF to Image Converter, available through the Google Play Store for Android phones. It is free and will turn your PDF into a JPG file for you. You then need to go to the documents upload section of the Driver App you are using. Then, if you are using an Android smartphone, go to your File Manager, and then click Local. Then locate PDFTOIMG folder and your JPG image will be in there. I do not use iPhone, but they will have similar Apps that do the same thing in their App Store. Taking and uploading a screen shot of the insurance document may risk rejection by the Private Hire Operator because of the bad image quality when the image is blown up in size to see on their big computer screens. Hence the reason why it is better, if necessary, to use an App to convert your PDF file to a JPG file.

Accountant

It is highly recommended that you employ the services of an accountant for calculating the right figures needed for your Self Assessment Tax Returns. Their knowledge of personal tax laws for small businesses will be valuable for you to save money by ensuring you are claiming every tax deductible business expense you are entitled to. Plus, their costs are also tax deductible as well. Therefore, having an accountant should pay for itself.

Chapter 3: Ready to Go
– *Time to Make Money!*

In this section, we will focus on the important things you need to know and what to do to make your Private Hire Driver business to be as successful and profitable as possible.

Driver Kit
Here is a list of items that I have in my car at all times. The list contains items that will help you to deal with almost every eventuality that you are going to come across in your Private Hire business.

- Phone Cradle
- Bluetooth phone earpiece
- Tescos Cotton Neutraliser Air Spray
- Dettol Neutra Air Freshener Spray
- Surface wipes
- Surface antibacterial spray
- Box of tissues or roll of quality toilet tissue paper

- Hand towel (to wipe windows)
- Fabric odour neutraliser spray
- Pens + notepad
- iPhone and Android chargers
- Toothbrush + toothpaste for personal hygiene
- Outdoor urinal bottle
- Heavy duty wheel wrench (to remove wheel bolts)
- Owner's Manual for the vehicle
- Basic tool kit (containing screwdrivers, adjustable wrench and pointed pliers)
- Spare set of lamps and fuses
- Clear tape

Ring Rider at Pick Up

When you arrive at your destination, unless you are doing a ride share, always call your Rider to confirm that you are at the pick up point. They really appreciate this. It generally encourages them to hurry up and does not affect your rating. It means that you are less likely to be unnecessarily hanging around.

Destination Confirmation (Important)

Always confirm with the Rider their destination. It adds to the confirmation you have the right Rider with you. I have had a few times people falsely claiming to be the Rider by getting into my car and trying to get me to change the destination. Always politely refuse and request that since they are the Rider, they will need to change the destination from their own phone. Fortunately, this is not common. However, sometimes, things do go wrong with Apps. So, if the destination cannot be changed by the Rider (and you have confirmed they are the genuine account holder), don't worry because when you get the Rider to their destination the App will confirm that you want to end the trip there and you will still get paid fully for the journey made. However, with ride sharing services, neither the Driver or Rider's App allows for either the pick up or the drop off locations to be changed because these services are for fixed fares in advance only.

If the Account Holder has requested a booking for someone else and the destination needs to be changed, then you can confirm through the App by telephone or text the change requested. At the end of the day, you may need to use your discretion. I once had an App account holder that pre-booked a car for their friend to go to Heathrow Airport, but the destination said somewhere in Central London. Upon speaking with the account holder, they said that they could not change the destination (probably because of a technical problem on the App they were using). I have had this several times before, and I could not change it from my side either. So, I decided to use my discretion. I completed the trip at the Airport, got paid for that and then got another trip from the Airport because the App for that particular platform operator, recognised I had dropped off my last Rider at the Airport.

Sat Nav – Pros & Cons
There are clear differences to how the various SatNavs work. Google Maps and Waze are both owned by Google. Waze information feeds into Google Maps. The fastest App to load up is Waze, but it will take you down lots of back roads (including those with speed bumps). Google Maps generally

shows you clearly where there are road blocks. Waze does not always do that.

When starting off as a Private Hire Driver, for the first 3 months, I would strongly suggest that you set the Driver App to use either Waze or Google Maps because the App platform operator's SatNav may not be as up to date as either Waze or Google Maps. Therefore, it may be best to only use the Driver App SatNav once you are familiar with the roads in the area you are working. Otherwise the Driver App SatNav may take you down roads you are not meant to go into and cause you to unnecessarily get a Penalty Charge Notice. Therefore, you will need to use a lot of common sense and caution when using them.

If you can manage without having to use either Waze or Google Maps, then it is better because jobs load up faster using the Driver App only. However, if the journey is either more than 5 miles or the destination needs to be reached by a certain time, it may make sense to use Waze or Google Maps to ensure the route selected is most advantageous to the Rider. Sometimes, Riders may specifically ask you to use Waze. That is their choice and it needs to be respected. Personally, I think that Google Maps is far more superior than Waze, but it does take slightly longer to load up.

SatNav Problems

Every town and city have their poor mobile reception areas for either GPS or data. London is certainly no different. The tall buildings at Canary Wharf, as well as some parts of the City of London and City Road (Old Street area) can interfere with your SatNav GPS signal. Therefore, when entering an area where there is a known poor mobile reception problem try as much as possible to remember where your SatNav told you beforehand to pick up and drop off your Rider.

GPS signals are notoriously weak, and the GPS signals can get easily blocked. It may sound a bit obvious, if you have an external protection casing that you put your phone in to, try removing it, then go for a drive to test the SatNav and see it that solves your weak GPS signal problem. If it doesn't and your phone is still under warranty you should return it to the place you got it from. There are also many articles and Youtube videos on the internet suggesting fixes and work arounds for bad GPS signals, but these are at your own risk. At the end of the day, this is your livelihood, so if you do think you are experiencing serious issues with the GPS sensor in your phone you may need to consider getting a replacement phone altogether.

Finally, before getting a new or second hand phone, my suggestion is, wait at least 6 months after its initial launch date to find out if anyone has experienced any GPS problems with it. For example, you can put into Google search *[make and model of phone] GPS problems* and then see what comes up. If it passes that little test, then hopefully it should be okay to use it for private hire driving work. Also, by waiting for around 6 months after the initial release date of the phone, it may mean that you pay less for it because the initial demand will have died down considerably by then.

Airports – Drop off and Waiting
If you drop off a Rider at any of the Airports with Uber, and then click in the App as if to go to the Private Hire designated

waiting area, Uber will then prioritise you with a preferential position in the queue. There is no guarantee that you will get a return pre booking from the Airport. It depends on how busy at the time the App is. If you do not get any pick ups, then it will be better for you to come back towards Central London, by keeping to main urban roads and avoiding Motorways if you can. By doing this, it increases your chance of picking up some Riders on the way back. As an example, from Heathrow Airport consider using the A4 back to Central London, rather than the M4.

However, if you are using the Uber Driver App and choose to wait at an airport, then you will have to join the queue in the Private Hire Driver waiting area, which is often a waste of time. Many drivers do wait at airports and swear by it, but I disagree. I think it is better to be on the road making money rather than hoping for a big airport job that may not be that big because a Rider may not be going that far anyway.

TfL Emails

If you are working in London, look out for emails that come from TfL. They will often give essential information about vehicle journeys that would be affected by road closures. This is particularly important if road closures are the result of marches and demonstrations. It can affect a whole area. It may be better in some cases to avoid the area entirely, for both you and your Rider's sake.

Also, look out for both radio and television news travel information – this could include major streets closed off because of emergency gas and water works. Try your best to avoid these areas as much as possible. You could also set your radio to give you regular travel updates. Riders generally do not mind this.

Breaks
Do take regular breaks. This avoids having accidents due to inevitable tiredness. Try to avoid eating strong smelling foods. If you do, maybe consider either brushing your teeth or rinse your mouth with mouthwash after eating. This is because cars are closed spaces and you will have to breath out in the same space that they will have to breath and smell into.

Water
Unless you are doing executive trips, only keep water for yourself. Or give your Rider water free of charge if they feel unwell, that's a very nice and good thing to do. If the Ride is an executive type Rider, you will naturally be expected to provide water to your Riders free of charge anyway. But if the Ride is an ordinary pre-booked journey you are not obliged to provide it. Also, your Riders are not likely to give you better ratings or tip you extra for giving them water either. Instead always offer to drive past a shop so that they can go and buy water. They won't. They never do. So, this should say it all. But it is your profits and up to you.

Eating and Drinking
Never eat and drink in front of a Rider, it looks unprofessional and they may give you a bad rating. If you need to have a sip of water because your mouth is very dry or because you need to clear your throat just be discreet. Having a boiled sweet discreetly is ok. However, if you do need to eat something quick because of diabetes or need a sweet to keep

you going, just explain to your Rider, this will be completely ok and understandable.

Litter Rubbish
Always put all rubbish in public bins. It is against the law to throw or leave rubbish on the street. Never leave your rubbish behind, always take it with you until you can safely dispose of it.

Toilet
If you need to go to the toilet, always try first to use a publicly accessible toilet. TfL do provide a list on their website, but most of the toilets on the list are impractical without having to pay a parking charge. If you need to go, and there are no toilet facilities nearby then do so discreetly by using an 'outdoor urinal bottle'. They are available to buy through Amazon or Ebay. After each use, empty the bottle down a drain. Drains are spaced out along the roadside, generally within 100 to 200 metres of each other. After each use, spray the outdoor urinal bottle in and out with antibacterial surface spray and odour neutraliser air spray. Wash the bottle thoroughly at the end of each shift. Always store the bottle, wrapped in a bag, under the boot area of your car.

Combating Tiredness
Changes in body rhythm produce a natural increased tendency to sleep at two parts of the day: midnight to 6am and 2pm to 4pm. Also, working very long hours or after eating a very large meal can make you naturally sleepy and tired.

Therefore, do not drive if you are feeling tired. Do not take any more Rides. Tiredness kills. If you are tired, it is better to turn off the Driver App you are using, stop and pull over for a power nap (for maybe 10-30 minutes) or go home early. Better to have a break than risk having an accident (which risks lives and your livelihood).

Taking a cup of coffee or tea and then having a 10 minute nap while waiting for the caffeine to take effect may also assist. Boiled sweets, though are not healthy and good for your teeth, are good at keeping the mind active, but their effects are very short lasting. However, sometimes Riders may ask if you have a sweet or mint, so it can be good to have some with you. An alternative could be sugar free chewing gum if this can be chewed discreetly when you are carrying Riders. Fruits, such as apples and bananas are also good (and healthy), but again, offer very short relief.

Hayfever
If you think you may suffer from hayfever, you should always seek appropriate professional medical advice. They may recommend that an antihistamine may be beneficial for you. However, always READ the side effects warning with these medications. Some antihistamines may bring on tiredness or cause a mild seizure. All antihistamines have different side effects. It all depends on the brand and type you use. Therefore, it makes sense to always read the leaflet of any medication before using it.

Back Pain Problems
With long hours behind the wheel, working as a Private Hire Driver, can lead to serious back pain problems, because of the

way car seating maybe designed in the car being used. Always adjust your seat to ensure you are in an ergonomically comfortable position as possible. However, if you suffer from any kind of back problems, you should seek appropriate professional medical advice or assistance. I use a back support belt, which is about 7 inches (18 cm) wide and wraps around my waist. But this may not be appropriate for you. Therefore, you need to seek a medical professional who will be able to advise something specific to your own circumstances.

Odour Neutralising Air Spray

Tescos Cotton neutralising air spray is great. The Riders really love it. It is an excellent odour neutraliser. Riders will comment that the car smells fresh and clean, and generally always rate you positively for it! Use it regularly, maybe 2-3 times a day, especially when you have a Rider that may smell a bit.

Air Con System Smells

I also use Dettol Neutra Air Freshener spray as a back up de-odourising air spray. This spray is also a useful low cost way for fumigating and cleaning out the Air Con system. You can do this by turning on the engine and the Air Con at full blast. Then outside, under the windscreen wipers, where the air flows into the car Air Con system, spray about half a can of Dettol Neutra Air Freshener spray in there. It should make a lot of difference in getting rid of unwanted smells coming in through the Air Con system.

Hybrid Cars – Air Con

If you use a hybrid and drive it in economy mode all the time, using the Air Con, can run the battery down. Therefore, while you use the Air Con it may be better to not have the engine running in economy mode.

Anti-bacterial Multi Surface Wipes

Having a pack of anti-bacterial multi surface wipes is essential. They help you with your own hygiene as well as deal with any small messes that needs to be quickly cleared up without having to take your car fully off the road.

Box of Tissues

Always good to have a box of tissues or roll of toilet tissue paper available for your Riders to help themselves. I always keep a reasonable quality toilet tissue roll in the driver door compartment. It is handy if Riders have a bit of a runny nose or are tearful about something. Alternatively, you could get a simple small pack of 10 tissues.

Owner's Manual

The Owner's Manual for the vehicle you are driving should always be kept in the vehicle at all times. It contains basic information on maintenance, such as engine oil type, tyre pressures, how to change lamps and fuses (with locations and diagrams), as well as the meanings of warning lights on the dashboard, etc. If you own your own car and you do not have an Owner's Manual for it, you can either buy a cheap replacement hardcopy on Ebay or usually be able to download it free of charge from the internet.

Basic Tool Kit

Good to have in the car in case of any very small repairs that need to be done while out working. Your basic tool kit should ideally have at least a set of screwdrivers, adjustable wrench and pointed pliers in it. I had a car that the boot did not open because the electric connection wire that releases the latch lock broke. I also owned the car, so I had no choice but to fix it myself. I had to look up on the internet to figure out (a) how to get the particular make and model for my boot open from the inside of the car, and (b) how to fix the problem. I was able to fix the broken wire by rejoining the broken ends through a cheap connector I bought from an electrical shop. I was then back to work within an hour. You can get a cheap basic tool kit or tools separately from either Ebay or Amazon or any good auto accessories store.

Spare Lamps and Fuses
Good to have a spare set of lamps and fuses for the make and model of the vehicle you are driving. If the Owner's Manual for the vehicle is not available, then you may be able to find out quickly on the internet how to change your lamps and fuses, and where to locate the fuse box(es). You can easily check the fuses by removing them to see if any are blown. I had an incident where my car charging port (cigarette lighter) was not working. I found the location of the fuse box and a diagram for it through looking on the internet. I quickly changed the blown fuse and was then up and running, making money again within the hour.

Tyres – Punctures and Replacements
You may have noticed on the list of the Driver Kit at the beginning of this Chapter is 'heavy duty wheel wrench'. You can get this from either Ebay or Amazon or from any good motor accessories store. If you want a breakdown recovery service like the AA or RAC to help you because you have a puncture, they may not consider such requests as being

urgent. It may therefore take them up to 3 hours for one of their specialist tyre fitting and repair vans to come out to you. It is always better to therefore know how to change a wheel yourself. There are plenty of short 5-6 minutes videos on YouTube that can show you how. Changing a wheel will only take you around 20 minutes to do.

Replacing a tyre with a second hand one usually costs between £25 and £35 (maximum). Brand new budget tyres usually start from at least £70 each. If you have a puncture on the road, it may be worthwhile checking to see if there are any tyre repair and replacement fitters near you. You can check this by making a simple search by typing in 'tyres' into Google Maps and see what comes up. If you do drive on a flat tyre and the police stop you, they could prosecute you for driving a vehicle in an unfit condition, especially if the tyre was bald in the first place!

If you are having to drive with your spare wheel, my advice would be <u>do not work</u>, until you can change the tyre. If you have a Rider and you are in the middle of nowhere and you have a puncture, you will cause a great amount of annoyance and inconvenience to the Rider if they are stranded with you. A Rider once told me that it happened to them and they were very unhappy with the Driver as a result.

Wheel Bolts
If you notice any wheel bolts that need changing or you need to replace any wheel bolts you can buy replacement bolts at Halfords or Euro Car Parts or any good motor accessories store. Also, if you need to replace the locking bolt secure key then you can do that for around £25 at the relevant car dealer

for your vehicle, or if you know the number of the secure key you can order online through evoautomotive.com.

I have twice had problems with not being able to remove the locking bolt secure key due to it being worn out. I had to take the vehicle to a welding specialist garage. My mechanic welded an ordinary wheel bolt on top of the locking bolt so it could be naturally screwed off. The other way is for the offending bolt to be drilled out. Prevention is better than this fiasco any day!

How to Deal with Vomiting Incidences

Dealing with a vomiting incident (a Rider being sick in your car) is going to happen to you at some point. So, you need to prepare for it! All App based platform operators take things like vomiting very seriously and treat them as a matter of bad Rider behaviour. For instance, Uber will charge the Rider a fee of £50 + cleaning valet charge. But you will need photo evidence plus a car wash cleaning receipt. Other App based platform operators all have similar policies.

When I have a Rider who has been drinking, I generally always tell them in a very clear voice, *"If you need me to pull over for any reason, please let me know."* They really do understand what I am talking about, and it generally gets their attention! On the other hand, some Riders who may suffer from motion (travel) sickness and tend to discreetly unwind the window where they are sitting. In which case, much more attention to smoother braking, slower speeds and going more smoothly over road speed bumps will make a lot of difference to them to enjoy their trip with you better.

Below are some real life example stories of Riders from my own experiences of them making a mess that may help you to deal with such situations for yourself:

1.   I had a Rider with a friend, both were doctors returning home early from an evening out. But one of them was not feeling well and suddenly vomited, fortunately, outside of the window. After parking the car, the companion to the one who had vomited was able to help her. The mess on the outside of the window was awful. But I was able to use lots of toilet roll tissue paper, antibacterial multi surface wipes and antibacterial surface spray to give the door and surrounding area a good clean up. I then used odour neutraliser spray to ensure no smells were evident. Job done! No sign of the offending vomiting or any smells. I got both Riders home, they gave me a generous tip and I was able to work unaffected for the rest of the evening. Case closed.

2.   I had a Rider that vomited in my car and the mess was too much to clear up because some of it went on to both the seating and floor area. Therefore, I had to take the car out of service. They gave a tip for saying sorry and would accept any charge that Uber would send them. I took the car out of service, took photos and got an appropriate cleaning receipt. The Rider was charged £50 + £20 for the cleaning receipt.

3.   I had a Rider, very late at night, who urinated on the seat. I had no choice but to take the car out of service. The moment I got back home (at 1 am) I had to clean and fumigate the car seating area immediately, because if I let it dry then the urine would go into the fabric of the seating and I would never be able to get rid of the smell. But I felt a bit

sorry for the Rider because it was quite an unusual incident and she may have had a weak bladder because of medical reasons. I therefore decided to just let it go and put it down to one of those things.

4.   I had a couple of young Riders (male and female, about 17 years old). This was only about 6.30 pm in the evening. They looked responsible and were on their way to their school prom night. The female threw up, mostly out of the window. I did not know they had been drinking beforehand. After dropping them off at their school, I took the car out of service. I cleaned out most of the vomit at the scene (as above). I then cleaned the affected parts of the interior properly immediately I got home. I decided not to charge them because of their age. They apologised anyway.

"Keep Calm and Carry On"
This slogan comes from a famous Ministry of Defence, Second World War poster in 1939. The message for us Drivers in this generation should be:

- Always be quick to listen, slow to speak and slow to become angry in all circumstances. It's a Biblical command (James 1:19).
- Always conduct both your manner and attitude with absolute professionalism at all times.
- Do not use any form of bad language, abuse or threatening behaviour.
- Do not get involved with any confrontation with other road users.
- Do not use your horn in an aggressive manner.

- Never under any circumstances get out of your car, except to assist a Rider or attend to an accident.

- Do not lower your driver window more than 4 inches (even in hot weather). This is for your safety, and to ensure that your mobile phone is not stolen.

- Always keep calm and never react. If you do then your Rider will not feel safe, and they are more likely to give you a bad rating regardless of who's fault it is.

Rider Falling Asleep

Riders will commonly fall asleep in your car, especially after a late night out. They will often quickly wake themselves up when they are close to their destination or by you simply calling out their name. It is fortunately very uncommon that a Rider falls into a deep sleep in your car. I have only ever had this once, and they eventually came around after about a minute by themselves. If you are in this situation, never touch them to wake them up. Try calling out their name, giving their mobile phone a call or putting the radio on. If this still fails to wake them up, you may have to call the police.

Lost Property

If you find any lost property, always do your best to get it back to the owner. Unfortunately, you will not always get a tip for it. But it will at least save you the bother of having to drop the item off at the Private Hire Operator's office. You should always follow their instructions on what you should do with property left by a Rider.

App Operator Support

Mistakes with fares do happen. So, if you need to challenge a fare with any of the App based platform operators, always be polite and professional when explaining why you think a mistake has happened. You are more likely to get a positive response. Also, if you encounter any problems or do not understand anything, do let them know. Also, do read all emails they send you. That way you can keep ahead of any incentives, promotions, App developments and improvements they are doing.

Chapter 4: Ratings

Many drivers are rightly concerned about the ratings they receive from their Riders. This is because, if it goes below a certain level your account on the Driver App you are using may be deactivated. This is the case with Uber, if your rating falls below 4.5 stars. If you put the things you will learn in this Chapter into practice your ratings will always be consistently very high.

Rating Riders

At the end of every journey, always give your Rider positive feedback whenever possible by telling them you will give them 5 stars. This may remind them to do the same for you. You will need to do this to mitigate against inevitable negative ratings. If you consistently do this, you will able to cope with having 1-2 negative ratings out of every 30-40 Riders that rate you, and still maintain a reasonable rating. However, if you put the hints, tips and suggestions featured in this book your personal rating will be one of the highest and will consistently remain in the 4.90s.

Reasons for Negative Ratings

Your ratings as a Private Hire Driver on any of the App platforms are determined by your Riders satisfaction of the trip. This is, obviously, an entirely subjective rating. For instance, with Uber, after each ride, the Rider can credit you between 1 to 5 stars. 4 stars and below are regarded as negative. 5 stars are neutral. The most common reasons for receiving negative ratings are:

- Driving (driving too fast, going over speed bumps roughly, going through red traffic lights, braking to hard)
- Navigation (bad route)
- Vehicle untidy/unclean (also includes unpleasant smells and exterior damage or looking dirty)
- Bad driver hygiene
- Inappropriate communication (bad language or discriminatory or demeaning or sexual comments, arguments, etc)
- Harassment (trolling or inappropriate physical contact)
- Level of Service (this is a bit of a catch all but nonspecific reason)

Below are loads of hints, tips and suggestions to ensure your earnings and personal ratings remain high. Also, a positive Rider experience increases your chances of being tipped as well.

Communication, Communication, Communication...

Good communication is the number one way of ensuring consistently high ratings from Riders. This cannot be repeated enough. Riders really do enjoy talking to their Drivers, and they like to do it in <u>English</u>. If English is not your strong point, then please do practice it at every opportunity. Otherwise your rating will suffer badly. Riders most of the time enjoy talking with their Drivers, and always reward good conversation with high ratings and sometimes tips as well. The key to knowing if your English is good: If you can speak a few sentences sufficiently clear enough for a person who is not from your country to understand you the first time round then you have no problem, and your English is already good enough.

Phone Charger leads: iPhone + Android

Phone charger leads are an almost guaranteed way of ensuring you get 5 stars. You will hardly ever be requested for an Android phone charger, but you will always be requested for an iPhone charger (usually at least once a day). So, it is very important to have a spare iPhone charger with you in the car at all times.

AUX Cable vs Bluetooth Connection

Having an AUX cable is not important because all modern cars these days have Bluetooth connection capability. Some Riders who either have had too much to drink or may simply feel they cannot listen to music at a reasonable level may strongly request that you put up the volume. If the volume requested is too high for you or will distract you from your driving just politely apologise and say you cannot do it.

Limiting the audio volume to the level that you are comfortable to drive with will not affect your ratings.

Personal Hygiene

Always wash/shower yourself clean every day. Bad hygiene will make you smell and will result in negative ratings. If you try to hide body smells with perfume and deodorants without washing yourself, Riders will still notice. Use a neutralising deodorant (non-smell) spray if you need to. Also use an odour neutraliser air spray for the car. Always carry toothbrush and toothpaste for yourself. Also, always have a pack of anti-bacterial multi surface wipes for your hands. Lastly, if you have low-cost multiple access gym membership you can access washing and shower facilities when you need them, 24 hours a day. There are a lot of these gym facilities now.

Clothing

Always dress reasonably smart casual but tidy. That is, ideally a shirt and jacket/blazer (tie optional). No jeans or T shirts. This makes a very good business impression for Riders, and they appreciate it. Avoid wearing attire that is not associated with the European context. Otherwise it may look strange and unsettling for the Rider.

Phone Calls

Do not receive phone calls unless it is your spouse. Riders do not like it. Do not do it even if you have Bluetooth. If it is your spouse and you are very quick and brief, your Rider may even respect you for it. Riders will generally ask if they can either take or make phone calls. Always say yes, because it will help your rating.

Car Washing

Get your car washed (in and out) at least once or twice a week (or more, if necessary). Otherwise, your Riders may negatively rate you for having a dirty car.

When you need to get your car washed and you are outside your normal area, then open up the Google Maps app and type 'car wash'. You will then see all the hand car wash places near your location.

If you hire your car, and it is the first time you are using it, make sure before you start, to give the car seats a good wipe down with antibacterial wipes, as well as using a good fabric odour neutraliser throughout.

Cold and Hot Weather

Try to be conscious of how temperature fluctuations in the car can be affected by the weather outside as well as the temperature in the car. Do try to take into account that the temperature at the back of the vehicle can be generally different to the front. Also, different Riders have different cold and hot tolerances. So, it will take experience to find out what works best in your car. Do ask your Rider if they are happy with the temperature. This could be very good feedback at times, especially when the weather outside is exceptionally hot or cold.

Smoking

Do NOT smoke or use vaper e-cigarettes in your car. The smell stays around for quite a few minutes afterwards. Also, the smoke will stain the fabric of the seating and the ceiling of the vehicle. The smell will be hard to remove. If you need to smoke, then park up somewhere and get out of your car. This all sounds very over the top and also very inconvenient when it rains. However, your Riders will know you have been smoking and they may likely rate you negatively because of it.

Car Smells

Use a good odour neutralising air spray. Use it 2-3 time a day because its effectiveness quickly goes after about 45 minutes.

Chapter 5: How to Start A Conversation with A Rider

Conversations with Riders

We all have our own way of communicating. Some people do seem to be 'natural socialisers'. They can go around a room of people and have what appears to be deep meaningful and fulfilling conversations with every person there. They are the kind of people that look like they have so many friends and are accepted by everyone. However, the reality is very different. Yes, it is perfectly true that some people do seem to have a knack at being able to speak to almost anyone. But the vast majority of our conversations everyday are largely superficial or light. "How are you?" "When was the last time you went to the theatre or cinema, and what did you go to see?" "How is your wife/husband?" "What work do you do?" "Do you have any holiday plans this year?" So, you can see that with very little effort required, it can be very easy to get a conversation going at any level. If you are not sure how best to get a conversation going then this chapter is written especially for you.

So how do you start a conversation? There are more than 250 plus languages that are spoken in London. Throughout the world, when people have different languages separating them, they most often opt for English so that they can speak to each other. This is very obvious here in the UK. Someone from China and someone from France will speak to each other in English. You would think that the people who speak English as their first language must therefore have it easy. I think that they clearly do! But what if your first language is not English? Or what if you are a bit shy in not knowing what to say or how to say it? This chapter will help you.

If you do struggle with speaking English, then when you start any conversation make sure you speak slowly and clearly. This will help you to get the right pronunciation and build up your confidence. Also, Riders will not mind you speaking slowly. They will respect you more because you are clearly making an effort to learn to speak English. They may even help you. Practice speaking the letters of the alphabet and numbers. Think about and practice the syllable sounds in words. You could practice by simply reading out loud something in English, such as news articles you are interested in from BBC News Online from your smartphone. Find out what words mean. Look up their meaning/definition using Google. Then practice them.

Initial conversation starters you can use:
- *"How are you?"*

- *"How is your day going?"* or *"Have you had a good day?"*
- *"The weather is looking nice and sunny today, do you think it will last?"*
- *"Have you just finished work?"* or *"Are you in between meetings now?"*

It is always very good to ask open ended questions, because they make a conversation happen very easily. Try:

- *"What kind of books / movies do you like to read or recommend?"*
- *"How did you start getting into your current work / trade?"*
- *"How did you start your business?"*
- *"If you were not doing the job you do right now, what would you like to have done instead?"*

Fun open questions:

- *"If you ended up on a deserted island which 3 things would you take with you?"*
- *"Where would be your dream location holiday be if money was no object?"*

Exploring questions:

- *"What plans have you got for the weekend?"*
- *"Have you lived in London for long?"* also *"What do you like about living in London?"*
- *"What would you advise it takes to be successful in business?"*

More conversation tips:

- Do start (if you can) with initial eye contact or look at them in the mirror. They will see you look at them.

- Do smile at initial contact, it brings warm welcoming feelings.
- Don't ever touch the Rider
- Don't look at the Rider when you are talking to them and driving (except for brief glances in the mirror)
- Don't talk to them, if they give you short 2-3 worded answers. They clearly do not want to talk.
- They may tell you they do not want to talk or they need to work or need to make a phone call. In which case, leave them alone.
- You can get some good ideas from Google by searching: *conversation starter questions.*

Dealing with Controversial Subjects

When having discussions with your Riders, you may have already been told that you should avoid discussions on Politics – Religion – Sport. Having said that, it is up to you, but don't get rigid and uncompromising. Keep all conversations light and neutral, unless the Rider is particularly interested to hear your view. Before, you give your view, try to find out what their view is first and find a neutral position if you think that your own view could cause offense.

Never, ever use bad language or profanity. Be always respectful in your conversations with your Riders about all matters to do with religions, cultures, lifestyles, political beliefs and opinions. Always avoid controversial moral issues. It would be better to say that you do not have a view on some controversial subjects. For instance, the Bible instructs that judgment is not required against people of the world. So, it is better to say you do not have an opinion. Otherwise, taking a view on a sensitive controversial issue could be very easily misinterpreted as being offensive by the Rider and they may report you to the Private Hire Operator you are with, and in turn could be reported to TfL. A neutral response could be, "Sorry, I don't have an opinion." "It's a free country." "Sorry, I don't have a view beyond that." In short, be very careful of all sensitive controversial subjects so that you do not risk causing offense or getting suspended from the Driver App you are driving on and then risk losing your livelihood. There are a lot of very sensitive people out there, and their views too should be respected.

Sexual Harassment
Never engage in inappropriate conversations. Do not ask for phone numbers or email addresses or other contact details. If they report you, the Private Hire Operator you are driving for may take disciplinary action against you.

Do not keep looking at your Rider. Or look at their body in anyway. They may interpret it as sexual harassment and report you. TfL have a zero tolerance of such behaviour and may revoke your license. Do not judge the way someone dresses. Just do your job and get paid. That is the bottom line of why you are doing what you are doing. Just remember that the reason why a Rider is riding with you is because they believe that the App platform you are driving for will take them safely to their destination. Therefore, Riders are entitled to feel safe with you at all times.

Physical Contact

Never physically touch your riders under any circumstances, unless they reach out to shake your hand or actually say they need assistance.

Chapter 6: Minicab Private Hire Companies – *Cash Work*

Besides the App based platform operators like Uber, Viavan, Kapten, Bolt and Ola, there are hundreds of big and small traditional operators. Many of which have been around before the internet. Some of these you may have seen around, such as Addison Lee, Carrot Cars, Greyhound, GLH, Green Tomatoes and Data Cars (to name a few). Along with these companies are hundreds of local minicab firms. All these Private Hire Operators may have contracts or agreements with local authorities, supermarkets as well as corporate and private individual accounts. Though many of these are moving towards more sophisticated App based platform solutions to compete with the existing App based platform operators. Many Private Hire Operators may have an App for their customers to download and use to request a minicab, but use a separate App for their drivers called Cordic (by the software development company of the same name). The

Cordic App is an off the shelf system that can be easily tailored to suit the needs of an individual Private Hire Operator.

Type of Vehicles

Most Private Hire Operators deal with 5 and 7 seat vehicles. However, some operators, like chauffeur services, are focused exclusively on providing executive vehicles only. Others may deal with a mixture. Some cars like the Toyota Prius Plus that have 7 seats are treated by Uber as UberX (5 seats) only, but local minicab firms will accept these as 7-seater cars. You will be able to do more jobs if you have a 7-seater vehicle. Large estate type vehicles are attractive because of picking up family shopping and airport runs. The bigger the vehicle the more work you will be able to do. However, if you have a van type multipurpose 8 seat vehicle you will not be able to drive through the Rotherhithe Tunnel because of height restrictions. Black Taxis are exempt from this restriction.

Which Operator to Drive For

You can find out which ones are recruiting by going to Gumtree or one of the many online recruitment sites like, Monster, Reed and Indeed. Also, you can contact many of the Private Hire Operators mentioned above through their websites, because all of them are constantly looking for new Drivers. You may need to try some of them and see how you get on. Each have their pluses and minuses. Driving for bigger operators mean you are less likely to be driving back to base empty. Also, many of the smaller operators are linked to back end online platforms that mean jobs they cannot fulfil themselves can be given to other operators. This too, helps to reduce the chance of their drivers coming back to base empty.

My advice is that if you wish to drive for any of these companies that you do open shift only and also drive for one or more of the App based platform operators as well. That will allow you to be flexible in your work times and ultimately earn more.

You are also more likely to get airport runs from these types of companies. This is because there are popular Rider based Apps that allow operators to bid on airport and other Rider requested jobs. If you want to do airport jobs, then it makes sense to drive for companies that operate closer to them. West and South West London is particularly good for this, because Private Hire Operators who have their office based there are more likely to do a higher amount of pick and drop offs at London Heathrow and Gatwick.

Cash and Account Work

All these companies will do a mixture of Cash and Account Work. Local minicab firms may typically do up 90% Cash work. Also, because of the higher level of cash work the tips that you get are significantly higher than compared with the App based platform operators, where payment is directly processed from the Rider's credit/debit card at the end of the journey.

Local minicab firms serve a wide variety of people from the area they operate in. Many of their customers may have to rely on the cash economy or may not have an account with any of the App based platform operators. Also, many of these local minicab firms have a strong loyal customer base, who simply like the personal service they feel they get, as well as having the same regular drivers drive for them when they ask for them by name.

What to Do When You Get a Rider Request

When you have accepted a Rider request from these types of operators always call the Rider and let them know you are on your way, how long you will be and, always ask them if they will be ready when you come. If you don't, they may either waste your time by not being ready at the pick up point when you arrive or delay you for other reasons. It is not uncommon to go on a 10-15 minutes journey only to be told that the customer has already left and gone with another minicab firm. That is why it is essential that you follow this advice so you can reduce the chances of your time being wasted and to maximise your earnings.

If the journey is particularly long, you may want to ask for the money up front. You are perfectly legally entitled to do that, and in some instances the minicab firm may expect you to do that as well. Also, if the customer says that they will pay at the other end because a cash machine is near where they are getting off, my advice is to stop along the way (particularly if you suspect the person has behavioural issues), because not all cash machines work (and also, the Rider may not actually have any money in their bank account to pay you). But that is at your own discretion and risk.

Cash based airport jobs through these types of Private Hire Operators rarely give you tips, because the work comes to the Private Hire Operator through one of the comparison Rider Apps out there, such as Minicabit, Kabbee and Cabubble. The way these Apps work is, Private Hire Operators bid on the

Rider requested journeys being posted on them. The reason why customers use them is that they hope to save money.

Airport Pick Ups and Drop Offs

There are five main international Airports that serve London. Heathrow, Gatwick, Stanstead, Luton and London City. Some charge the Drivers for dropping off, however, all of them charge for picking up.

It usually takes around 40 minutes for international travellers to come through to Arrivals from the time the plane has landed. For local flights this can be reduced to 20-30 minutes maximum. Therefore, before picking up a Rider at the Airport be mindful of this as well as importantly checking that their flight has landed. Otherwise you will find yourself paying extra on Airport parking charges. However, before good Operators send you to pick up from Airports, they will usually have checked for you the expected real time landing of the flight. Private Hire Operators usually refund their Drivers for the Airport parking charges if the Rider does not show up or cancels and it is not the Driver's fault.

London Heathrow Airport currently has 4 out of the 5 Terminals working. Drop offs are free. Before going into Arrivals to meet your Rider, you will need to park your car. For Terminals 2, 3 and 4, my strong advice is to park your car on Level 1 for easy access to Arrivals. For Terminal 5, any of the Levels 4-1 is ok, but not Level 0 (exit only).

Gatwick and London City drop offs are also free. However, you have to pay for parking to pick up. Stanstead and Luton charge Drivers when they do both drop offs and pick ups.

Chapter 7: Common Traffic Laws

In this chapter we will briefly take a look at the most common traffic offences and contraventions that many Private Hire Drivers get caught out with every day.

'Car Dooring'

This is a term that is used to describe a collision occurring when a bicycle or motorcyclist or any other road user collides into a vehicle door that has been opened by a vehicle occupant who did not look carefully before they opened their door. It is most common in urban built up areas. It is also a road traffic offence and causes around 500 accidents a year, in some cases fatal as well. A case went to court in 2017 when a mother of four, opened the taxi door behind the driver and a 26 years old cyclist hit the door, was knocked over and killed. She was prosecuted and given a £170 fine. The taxi driver was also prosecuted and fined for not warning the passenger in time. Car dooring is common, and I get incidences where Riders do not look properly before opening their car door and leading to cyclists at the last split second being forced to swerve out of the way.

<u>Please ensure you always tell your Riders to leave the vehicle on the pavement side</u>. Also tell them to always look and take care before they open their passenger door. You should always check it is safe for them to open the door by looking and checking your mirrors. Politely but firmly tell them not to open the door before you have given them the ok to do so.

Speed Cameras
Normally, speed cameras are set up to capture speed offenders when the speed is over Xmph + 10% + 2mph. For example, in a 40mph speed limit area a speed camera will capture images when a vehicle's speed goes over 46mph. However, a few are only set at the speed limit itself, and if you are caught then you will still be regarded as breaking the law. Please be aware also that Riders <u>do not like</u> being driven around fast. So always keep within the speed limit.

TfL and other London Boroughs have been actively working with the Metropolitan Police Service to bring around 700 speed and traffic light cameras into use. Of these, around 60 speed cameras are 20 mph. Not all of these cameras are enforced at present. However, more areas across London are being turned into 20 mph zones. Not seeing the speed restriction signs is not going to be a compelling defence in a Magistrates Court. If you are convicted of speeding, along with at least 3 penalty points you may also receive a substantial fine in the hundreds of pounds if it goes to court. So please drive carefully, and keep your driving license clean.

Phone Cradle position

Make sure that your phone cradle is either attached to the side of the window close to your side or attached to the air con grill. It is illegal to attach a cradle sucker to any part of the centre of the window. This is because it can block your view.

If you have not got one already, you would be well advised to get a Bluetooth Phone Earpiece, you can get a reasonably very good one from either Amazon or Ebay for less than £25. It is illegal to hold your phone while driving. Anyone caught either holding their phone or using it while driving may get 6 penalty points on their license.

Taxi Touting (Plying for Hire)

Taxi touting (plying for hire) is an illegal offence. If you are caught and convicted, the Magistrates Court will fine you and add 6 points on your driving license for no insurance, and you will also have your Private Hire Driver license revoked. Your hire and reward insurance is only valid by the insurers as long as you keep to the law and regulations of the principle authority that licensed you. Breaching this will mean you will not have any insurance in place. The police have a dedicated team who go out at night waiting to catch Private Hire Drivers doing it. They do this by having a person standing on a street late at night. They have to wait for a Private Hire Driver to approach them. Once a fare is discussed then the offence has been committed. Their police colleagues will surround the Private Hire Driver with their body cams on to take down evidence at the scene. I know this because I had a former Driver as a Rider to take to the Crown Court who was hoping to successfully appeal against his conviction at the Magistrates Court. I felt sorry for him, so I parked up the car and went in with him to offer moral support (and to learn and see what happens). Needless to say, he lost. The moral to this story is obvious, do not under any circumstances engage in any form of taxi touting (plying for hire). Only do pre-booked journeys through the Private Hire Operators you are registered with. Do not trust anyone. If you want to give anyone a free lift that is on you, but do not do it for money or any other reward.

Traffic Lights – Advance Stop Line
Never stop at traffic lights in the box with a cyclist sign on the ground. It is against the law and you could get prosecuted with up to 3 penalty points. However, if you have to stop in the box because the light turned orange when you stopped, you have not committed an offence.

Yellow Box Junctions
Yellow Box Junctions on Red Routes in London are under the enforcement control of TfL, otherwise they are enforced by local authorities. Some are CCTV camera enforced, many are not. If you stop in a Yellow Box Junction for 2 or more seconds, and it is enforced, then you will be at risk of getting a Penalty Charge Notice.

When entering a Yellow Box Junction, you are legally allowed to:

- Enter into it if the exit (other side) of the box is clear, or
- You are turning Right (as long as it is not at a roundabout or similar gyratory system).

It is a legal defence if you get stuck in a Yellow Box Junction because another vehicle cut in front of you and prevented you from exiting the box junction. The authorities know this, and therefore don't generally issue a PCN in this instance. Also, unless more than 25% of your car is in the box then, again, they may be unlikely to issue you with a PCN. This is because of something called the 'de minimis' principle. That is something that is too minor and trivial to merit consideration in law. I have had an appeal upheld on this as a legal defence due to my car catching just the tail end of the bus lane. But it is not an easy defence to make.

Picking Up and Dropping Off Riders – Street Restrictions and Regulations

You can pick up and drop off on red routes and bus lanes. Usually, TfL allow a grace period for up to 2-3 minutes maximum on a red route for Private Hire Drivers to pick up and drop off, but do put your hazard lights on. You must leave the Bus Lane within 3 car lengths. Do not park, pick up or drop off at zig zag lines or bus stop stands or taxi rank parking, otherwise you will definitely get a Penalty Charge Notice. If you already are familiar with the pick up location and you know that it is a crowded place or parking is highly restricted, try to call your Rider in advance to agree where you can meet them. Always put your hazard lights on when waiting for your Rider. It helps them to see and identify your car better, and also helps other road users to let them know to go around you. Also, parking on a zig zag line can get you 3 penalty points on your license.

Parking on Yellow Lines

If you park on a yellow line, you will only get a parking ticket if a parking enforcement officer is able to place a ticket on your car or give it to you, and take photos as evidence. The reality, however, is that if they see you in the car they are more likely to just leave you or simply tell you to move along, because otherwise you will drive away before they can put the ticket on your car and take the necessary photos as evidence.

Loading and Unloading Restrictions

Loading Bays on Red Routes are very common. They are enforced through CCTV cameras, and a lot of people get caught out by them. Do not park in them under any circumstances unless you are dropping off or picking up. Otherwise <u>you will</u> get a Penalty Charge Notice.

All Yellow Line roads, including those that that have Loading Bays, cannot be enforced by CCTV cameras, and require enforcement officers to physically issue you with a parking ticket. If you stop in one during the restricted times, do not leave your vehicle, otherwise you will get a PCN!

Taxi Rank

Do not park or pick up/drop off Riders at taxi ranks. Otherwise you will risk getting a penalty charge notice.

No Motor Vehicles Sign

No Motor Vehicle Signs generally have a car and a motorcycle in a red circle. They generally also have instructions to the restrictions, such as Pedestrians only, or Access only or set times when restrictions apply. Take care to carefully read the restrictions. They are generally heavily enforced through

CCTV by local authorities and bring a great amount of revenue to them.

No Entry Signs
These are circle signs that are fully filled in red with a white horizontal bar. The sign means that no entry to traffic under any circumstances. I have been caught by a CCTV camera going through a temporary No Entry Sign. No excuse. I am putting it here so you know that you should not ignore any signs, even the temporary looking ones!

No Left/Right Hand Turning
These signs are a very common and trap a lot of drivers. When you see them, please beware, because many of them have CCTV cameras looking out for drivers to catch.

Parking on Private Land
If you want to park on either a public car park or private land you should always pay. Always do read the conditions of parking on the posted notice boards around the car park. By parking there you are agreeing to their terms and conditions. You do however, have up to 10 minutes grace period from entering into a public or private land car park. This is to give you time to read the terms and conditions of parking on the land.

If you get a Parking Charge Notice from parking your vehicle on private land, and you want to make a Representation against it, then this is currently covered under the Freedom of Protections Act 2012, Schedule 4. It is very short but quite complex. When you do make your Representation to the parking enforcement company they are very likely to reject it every time, and you will then have to risk taking your Appeal to the Parking on Private Land Appeals (POPLA). They have lots of useful information on their website.

I appealed a Parking Charge Notice for staying too long at a McDonald's car park. I made a Representation using the Act on the grounds that the enforcement company did not enclose with the notice they sent me various documents including my hire agreement (as stated in the Act) because the car was hired. They rejected my Representation (as expected) but they lost at Appeal. In fact, they did not even contest it. Was I originally at fault? Yes, but the law is the law and it cuts both ways. Not everyone can have the patience to make the effort of an Appeal. However, it saved me £60!

Dealing with Penalty Charge Notices (PCN)
Every professional driver gets these. They are almost unavoidable. I get around 4-5 a year only. Local Authorities issue a great many PCNs to drivers because they have almost blindly followed their SatNavs into a restricted road. Blaming a SatNav is not a legal defence, and if you use it then your appeal is going to rightly be rejected. Do take care when Riders give you directions. If you know that entering a road is going to be illegal, then do NOT do it. None of the Private Hire Operators will help you if you get a PCN.

When you receive the PCN you will have 14 days to pay if you want to benefit from the discount. Currently, in London, this is £65 (50% discount of the PCN at £130). Always check the details on the PCN. Never assume it must be correct. Check the photos (and video) on the Authority's website. If you make a representation to the authority before the 14 days expire, then if they reject your Representation, they will give you a fresh 14 days to pay at the discount rate.

If your Representation is rejected by the Local Authority who issued the PCN, and you still feel you are in the right, then you will have to lodge an Appeal. If the PCN was issued in London, then you will need to lodge your Appeal with the London Appeals Tribunal Service. Appeals for PCNs issued outside of London are dealt with at the Traffic Penalty Tribunal. Both tribunal appeals services have lots of information as well as details of previous case examples on their website. The internet is also full of examples where cases have been won and Appeals being upheld against local authority councils. However, if you wish to go down this route, then my suggestion is that you will be able to make a much stronger case at the respective Appeals Tribunal if in London, you turn up in person or if outside of London deal with it over phone through a conference type call.